Just- For- Fun- Poetry

Camille Kay Bogle

Copyright© 2018 By James A Bogle
All rights reserved. Use of any materials or artwork found in this book is prohibited.
—
All Poems by Camille Kay Bogle
—
Cover design by James A Bogle
Edited by James A Bogle
—
Special thanks to
Nita Feliciano
Sonya Grayson

This Book Is Dedicated
to

Airami
Alosha
Alexis
Sean
Andrea
Skye
Danny
Wilnida
Jonathan
Patrick

Table of Contents

Weather Wise

What's Your Sign ?..6
Rain By Any Name..7
Category What?..8
Thar She Blows!...9
What's In A Name 10
Aftermath..11
Aftermath II...12
Let it Rain !...14
"Texas-Can-Do" State...15
Ode To Rain..16
Whale Of A Time..17
There's Always Weather..18

Hooray For Holidays !

Welcome, New Year!...19
Hoggin' The Spot Light !..20
Valentines, Everyone ?..21
Sure'n It's Paddy's Day..22
It's Mother's Day...23
Memorial Day...24
It's Father Time...25

4th Of July Let's Celebrate 26
Hallowe'en 'Tis the Witching 27
Pumpkins On Review..28
Thanksgiving A Most American Holiday........29
Happy Birthday, Yogi Berra................................30
Christmas! There's Nothing Like It !.................32

Philosophically Speaking

Spring Fever..33
Spring Preening, Anyone?...................................34
Living It Up (Not Down)..................................35
Pick And Choose...36
Accentuate The Positive......................................37
Spending Wisely..38
Computer Ease...39
A Special Gift...40
Humor Me, Please...42
Springtime At Last !..43
Think About It !...44
Simply Living...45
You're In Luck..46
It's Later Than You Think !..................................47

What's Your Sign?

The weather is always with us—
Just prepare for each change.
If the air was always the same,
It would soon feel very strange.

You might have already heard this:
There's a twenty percent chance of rain.
It's any weather-person's standby,
And there is nothing to explain!

So let's be cheery in December.
Let's be all a-bloom in May
Everyone has a favorite month—
To celebrate that next birthday.

Rain By Any Name

"It's a frog strangler" —
That means it's a rain.
Now it's re-strangling frogs,
Yes, you hear rain again.

If we had any gullies,
It's a gully washer, we'd say.
Maybe it's an epic storm—
We'll say so anyway.

Maybe it's a deluge
We'll wish for Noah's Ark.
There will be power outages—
Sometimes we are in the dark.

We followed our Grandpa's advice:
"Build on ground that's high"
So let it rain cats and dogs—
We are always snug and dry!

P.S
When it's a toad drowner,
Just don't go outside.
Unless you're in a boat
That rises with the tide.

Category What?

When a hurricane is named.
It's time to take note.
Get out the check list—
By now known by rote.

A pantry well-stocked,
Cases of water on hand.
Hatches battened down
Is the number one command.

Roof top stuff secured
So neighbors can relax.
Lanterns and flashlights
With batteries to the max.

Power outages are routine,
But radio usually comes thru.
Best advice is common sense,
And that's always up to you.

So if you are careful,
You don't have to fear
Thank goodness hurricane season
Only comes once a year!

Thar She Blows!

The wind is a-blowin';
The shutters are a-bangin';
The palm trees are swayin';
The wind chimes are clangin'.

It started out a category one—
Now it's up to five.
Numbers really don't matter,
It's just good to be alive.

The rain is horizontal,
And vertical as well.
Sounds like most everything
Is going straight to hell!

I'm sitting here sipping my drink,
And looking out my window pane.
Soon the sun will be shining.
This is not my first hurricane.

Epilog
But if I get another hurricane warning,
I'm going elsewhere pretty fast,
'Cause that Hurricane Maria
Is absolutely my very last!

What's In A Name

Don't name a baby Harvey—
It will only cause him pain.
Everyone will tell him
'Twas an awful hurricane.

Now Harvey, The Rabbit,
Is one we should revive.
Let's keep imagination
Totally well and alive.

Don't name a girl Maria—
Strike it off the list.
You can bet in Puerto Rico,
She will never be missed.

Maybe they'll return to numbers
For these yearly hurricane games
Before they use up
Any more of our favorite names.

Aftermath

Diggy lost half his house.
We didn't even lose the shed.
Some neighbors lost their awnings;
We just had good luck instead.

Everything down at the beach
Disappeared or washed away.
Perhaps a more pristine shore
Will be allowed to stay.

Recognize that generator hum?
It's the most encouraging sound.
But it's not the only thing running—
Everyone's hitting the ground.

People are pulling together—
Helping one another along.
There's now a new motto:
It reads" Puerto Rico Strong"

Aftermath II

Flashlights and lanterns
Are great against the dark,
But even gas appliances
Usually need an electric spark.

And remember the generator
Cannot run out of gas.
It may be a long time
Before "This Too Will Pass."

Better put up the clothes line,
Take advantage of the sun.
Start the job of clean-up;
There's plenty to be done.

Make use of the rainwater,
Save the good stuff to drink.
The word is this may go on
Much longer than you think.

Make no mistake about it,
This is not a children's game
Life here is Puerto Rico
Will never be the same.

P.S.
It will be a lot of work
To return green across the land,
Volunteers are always needed,
So come " Machete in hand!"

Let it Rain!

I love the sound of rain.
It often puts me to sleep.
Sometimes it makes me dance—
To pirouette and leap!

Those wind-splashed droplets
Across the windows glide
It feels so wonderfully good
To be snug and warm inside!

"Texas-Can-Do" State

They say such a storm
Happens every thousand years.
Let's hope that's really true—
'Twould be music to the ears.

It inundated Houston.
Rockport got the worst.
Everywhere needs responders—
Hard to say who's "first"!

Lots of independence in Texas,
And recovery is the mode.
Big jobs can use the help—
Joining in carrying the load.

When it comes to remembrance,
Some Times become renown,
And Texas will just never forget
When Harvey came to town!

Ode To Rain

When it starts to rain,
I really don't seem to mind.
I'll just put up my umbrella,
And get any rain gear I can find.

I might even do a dance,
That rite of spring in May.
Not that I need an excuse,
I like to dance every day.

Rain just freshens everything
And makes all green things grow
So rain now, and rain then—
Just don't let it snow!

Whale Of A Time

I once saw three blue whales
On a boat trip that I took.
I heard the Captain yell " See There!"
Twice more, he cried "Look ,Look!"

The ocean was so very blue
In those sunny southern climes,
But did I really see three whales,
Or just one whale three times!?!

There's Always Weather

When March comes along,
It seems like winter's end.
Putting spring into my step.
Everything's on the mend.

I feel like parading
Easter bonnet or not.
April's already in the air.
I look forward to being "Hot."

Having different seasons
Really is a design divine.
So let's welcome every single change
The weather? I say, "Just fine!"

Welcome, New Year!

Welcome, New Year! Welcome!
Let's give a cheer or two.
We're glad you did arrive;
There's a Welcome Mat for you

Say "Hello, year Two-Thousand- Plus"—
You'll surely put us to the test.
Let's make this year a good one—
Let's make it the very best!

Hoggin' The Spot Light!

There's a town in Pennsylvania,
Punxsutawney is its name.
That's where Phil the Groundhog
Plays out his annual game.

There will still be more winter
If his shadow's on the ground.
What did you just say?
It's the other way around?

Well I just have this one concern,
And it's my annual plight:
The name -PUNXSUTAWNEY—
I just hope to spell it right!

Valentines, Everyone?

Just when winter is " too much with us,"
Along comes a Valentine's Day.
And a card with a heart and flowers
Makes February seem like May.

It's a day for all kinds of lovers
Who can choose their bit of bliss.
My sentiments tend to go with
Those who grab a chocolate kiss!

Sure'n It's Paddy's Day

Who's to know if you're Irish or not
When Saint Patrick's Day rolls around.
It's fun to wear a shamrock,
And join the parade in town.

If you put an "O" apostrophe
In front of your very own name,
You may meet another Irishman
Who once did just the same.

Just say " Top o' the mornin' "
And "B'Gorey you're lookin' grand!"
Be sure to know that that " ole sod"
Means the isle that's Ireland.

It's time to put on something green,
And smile in that Irish way—
And give a cheer to one and all
On this great St. Paddy's Day!

It's Mother's Day

This is a very special day,
A salute to all the mothers
Who occupy that unique spot—
A place above all others.

Giver of advice and daily rules,
Plus wisdom, care and love.
Always encouraging excellence—
Yes, all the above .

To each a Happy Mother's Day !
Your hour is finally here.
But it's really saying "Thank you"
For every day of every year !

Memorial Day

To our Armed Forces– We salute you!
On this very special day.
To keep our country free,
We owe more than we can pay.

We can't forget nor time diminish
Your paying the ultimate sacrifice;
Giving your youth and valor
Is truly beyond any price.

To each branch of the Service,
And each one of the ranks.
We are proud to salute you
As we give our grateful thanks.

It's Father Time

Let's all give a cheer,
And say hip, hip, hooray.
To one special guy—
Yes, Happy Father's Day!

You may call him Dad:
Some even go for Pops.
Just be sure you tell him,
For you, he's The Tops!

4th Of July - Let's Celebrate !

Break out the flags—
Strike up the band.
The Fourth of July
Is nearly at hand!

Our American story
Is told far and wide.
This human spirit triumph
Ever fills me with pride.

But no resting on laurels;
The work isn't done.
Freedom's not for granted,
It's to be constantly won.

To keep our country safe,
Productive, strong, and free,
It takes every one of us,
And that means you and me !

Hallowe'en

'Tis The Witching Hour

The best part of Halloween
Is deciding what to be !
An eye patch makes a pirate,
Don a wig, and He's a She.

A broom identifies a witch.
If wearing a pointy hat
Try whiskers and a mask,
And you can be a witch's cat.

Devils and dragons are trouble—
The tail can slow them down,
Since top-notch " Trick-or-treaters"
Have to race around the town.

A little paint can make a clown.
Sheeted ghosts come short and tall,
But handing out the candy
Is the most fun job of all !

Pumpkins On Review

When Fall is the season,
Ripe pumpkins come to mind.
A perfect Jack-o-Lantern
Is one I hope to find.

Cinderella had a pumpkin-coach
To drive her all around,
And over in the pumpkin patch,
One might see Charlie Brown.

Then there's pumpkin- eater Peter
That someone did fantasize,
But the very best of pumpkins
Are turned into pumpkin pies.

Thanksgiving
A Most American Holiday

A time to count our blessings,
As we go along life's way
You can roast a turkey—
A big one would be wise;
Let's ask four and twenty friends,
And I will bake the pies.
Let's gather all the family,
And to each one, let's say,
"You are the biggest blessing!"
As we toast Thanksgiving Day!

Happy Birthday, Yogi Berra

Baseball legend Yogi Berra
Says that he never said
Half the things that others
Say that he ever said.

But studying up on Yogi
Is always time well spent.
No matter what he said
We all know what he meant.

"It gets late here very early"
No way could Yogi fake it,
And I follow his instructions
"At the fork in the road, (I) take it."

"The future isn't what it used to be"
Is profound as all "get out"
"A dime isn't worth a nickel anymore"
Gives one a lot to think about.

My favorite of his sayings
May be one you've heard before—
"That place is just too crowded,
No one goes there anymore."

Yes, Yogi's both wise and funny
And totally without pretense.
He's just that most uncommon person—
A MAN OF COMMON SENSE!
Happy Birthday, Yogi Berra!

Christmas!
There's Nothing Like It!

There's really nothing like it–
The excitement of a Christmas dawn.
Someone filled the stockings–
The milk and cookies gone.

There's really nothing like it–
The Christmas tree lit up,
Ornaments on every branch,
Holiday eggnog in a cup.

There's really nothing like it
To give the spirits a lift–
That wonderful beribboned package
That is a very special gift.

There's really nothing like it
On earth or in Heaven above
Like waking up to a Christmas
That's shared with those you love.

Spring Fever

Do I even want to get up?
That's sort of hard to say.
Is something really necessary?
What HAS to be done today?

Let's get a cup of coffee—
See how that makes me feel.
I'm sure there's nothing urgent—
I'm sure it's no big deal.

Maybe if I think some more
A purpose I will find.
I'd like to think I can affect
The powers that rule my mind.

So shall I just be lazy,
Take time off today and shirk?
Or just not try to think at all—
JUST GET UP AND GO TO WORK!

Spring Preening, Anyone?

Once again here comes spring
To put our hearts a-flutter,
But spring cleaning heads my list—
Getting rid of all that clutter.

It's not just hidden corners
That need a yearly cleaning.
"Cobwebs of the mind"— Begone !
Let's call it Spring Preening.

What better chance to say,
Non-collecting time is here!
Pass on, throw out, or even sell—
Make space YOUR New Frontier!

Living It Up (Not Down)

Now that I'm older,
I don't hurry much anymore.
I don't even notice things
I'm sure I used to see before.

I'm giving up sky-diving.
I'm considering a bucket list,
But there isn't much in life,
I figure I have missed.

Having little responsibility
Can be a very happy state.
I never get up early,
And I often get up late.

I even sometimes take advice,
And never, ever give it,
Except this one little bit–
"IT'S YOUR LIFE SO LIVE IT!"

Pick And Choose

If you join "Nitpicker's Anonymous,"
You'll make a lot of friends.
The motto is understandable
"Means don't justify the ends,"

They say " Pick your battles"—
And that's playing it very smart.
If you want a life " whole"-some,
Don't pick it all apart.

Give each and every person
A chance on his/her own.
You may never have to pick
So doggedly at that bone.

You've heard of "live and let live"—
The idea is quite well-known.
It's great advice to follow—
Or — go ahead— LIVE ALONE!

Accentuate The Positive

Having a positive attitude
Is surely half the game.
Soon everyone around you
Will be feeling just the same.

It leads to creativity
Of the hands and of the mind.
When you go along the right path,
The best is there to find.

Make life the most constructive;
Make being true your first reflex.
Make "Building up" a habit—
Call it your "Edifice Complex!"

Spending Wisely

Someone once wrote "Time you thief,"
And we know what that does mean.
It seems the days go flying by—
Never more to be seen.

Don't leave those needed words unsaid.
And don't forget it's fun to play.
Remember to count the blessings
That come along the way.

A special job in life should be
To plan how time is spent.
Never be the one that's saying,
"I wonder where it went!"

Computer Ease

Ever argue with a computer?
It's mostly a fruitless task.
Sometimes answers just don't match
The questions one did ask.

Technology holds great promise
Of making things easier to do.
Is there room for improvement?
Well I'm just asking you.

Young people learn so very fast.
No matter how you "Hew" it.
It's best to keep things simple.
So even grown-ups can do it.

A Special Gift

Everyone needs a special spot.
A place to take one's ease.
Maybe by the sound of water.
Or wind chimes murmuring in the breeze.

Happiness is not something
That's bought down at the store.
Sometimes even a million bucks
Wouldn't really get you more.

The secret to life is simple,
Or just turn that around.
The simple life is the secret.
At least that's what I've found.

Having a few too many things
Can use up every day,
And then before you know it,
They've stolen your life away.

What you have to do is choose,
It's always your call,
And it's well worth remembering
Time is the most precious gift of all.

Humor Me, Please

I often think that humor
Is the real spice of life.
The best of all the cures
When along comes the strife.

It may even be the glue
That holds the family together.
If it's fun when skies are blue.
It's a necessity in bad weather.

Without a sense of humor,
Surely the deals will break.
Humor sweetens everything!
It's the icing on the cake!

Springtime At Last!

Spring is a good time
To de-clutter up your life,
It can be the right way
To relieve stress and strife.

Real treasures are good keepers,
But make that just a few.
You'll feel much, much lighter,
Even brighter, saying " Who knew?"

Having all that extra space,
(And here's the secret clue),
It is the best possible way
To make room for what's new !

Think About It!

It's hard to describe
just how thinking comes about.
It's a mental exercise
Like mind-weaving in and out.

If we could just bottle wisdom,
A lot of time could be saved.
The way for an experiment
Would already be paved.

But perhaps there'd be no challenge,
If the work is already done.
I guess I'll keep on thinking–
Won't you join me in the fun?

Simply Living

To keep life simple,
You gotta be really smart.
To please yourself and others,
It takes work and a lot of heart.

I like to forge just straight ahead,
"Cause detours take their toll.
I like to know each step I take
Puts me nearer to my goal.

The trick's to love the journey,
Doing good along the way.
Makes for a life worth living
When you value every single day!

You're In Luck

When preparation meets opportunity,
Good luck may be the call.
But you might say being ready
Is not just luck at all !

We make choices every day,
So let's figure out the Game.
It's good to have a target–
Even better is good aim!

It's Later Than You Think!

Some people sing it—
"It's later than you think!"
But you can also just say it.
It happens to you in a blink.

You should figure out a goal—
What you really want to do.
And the answer to all that
Is absolutely up to you.

You may think it's too early.
And feel you're in the pink.
The hard part is deciding.
Mull it over, have a drink.

With that business decided
Have some fun and be sure to wink.
The big thing IS-BE HAPPY!
It's later than you think!

www.ingramcontent.com/pod-product-compliance
Lightning Source LLC
Chambersburg PA
CBHW070802050426
42452CB00012B/2466

ALL RIGHTS RESERVED. No part of this report may be modified or altered in any form whatsoever, electronic, or mechanical, including photocopying, recording, or by any informational storage or retrieval system without express written, dated and signed permission from the author.

AFFILIATE DISCLAIMER. The short, direct, non-legal version is this: Some of the links in this report may be affiliate links which means that I earn money if you choose to buy from that vendor at some point in the near future. I do not choose which products and services to promote based upon which pay me the most, I choose based upon my decision of which I would recommend to a dear friend. You will never pay more for an item by clicking through my affiliate link, and, in fact, may pay less since I negotiate special offers for my readers that are not available elsewhere.

DISCLAIMER AND/OR LEGAL NOTICES: The information presented herein represents the view of the author as of the date of publication. Because of the rate with which conditions change, the author reserves the right to alter and update his opinion based on the new conditions. The report is for informational purposes only. While every attempt has been made to verify the information provided in this report, neither the author nor his affiliates/partners assume any responsibility for errors, inaccuracies or omissions. Any slights of people or organizations are unintentional. If advice concerning legal or related matters is needed, the services of a fully qualified professional should be sought. This report is not intended for use as a source of legal or accounting advice. You should be aware of any laws which govern business transactions or other business practices in your country and state. Any reference to any person or business whether living or dead is purely coincidental.

Copyright © 2021

TABLE OF CONTENTS

Waking Up to Your Greatness   3

Myths You've Believed About Money   8

    Money Myth #1: Money Is Evil   11
    Myth #2: People Who Want Money Are Greedy   14
    Myth #3: There Is Not Enough Money   16
    Myth #4: I'll Never Make Enough Money   18
    Myth #5: If I Make More Money, People Won't Like Me   20
    Myth #6: I'm Just Fine Without Money   22

The Power of Your Mind: Having an Abundance Mindset   24

    Your Mind Controls Your Outcomes   26
    Changing Your Mind About Money   29
    Opportunities Are Everywhere   31

Taking Action on Your Dreams   34

    Step #1: Write Your Dreams Down   36
    Step #2: Start Taking Action on Your Dreams   40

Your Dreams Are Waiting for You   42